THE
ODYSSEY
OF *My Life*

REV. JOSEPHAT CHAPONDA BANDA

The United Methodist Church Minister

All Scripture quotations are taken from the New International Version, NIV Study Bible.

ISBN: 978-1-39991176-4

DEDICATION

This book is dedicated to my beloved spouse, Mrs Mavis Banda, and our nine children: Mr Mulephere Banda; Dr Emmanuel Banda; Mrs Marcia Nkomo; Mr Ransom Banda; Mr Habakkuk Banda; Mrs Deborah Mawere; Mrs Tisungane Muganiwa; Mrs Thokozani Chiwara and Mr Shadreck Banda. Shadreck encouraged me to narrate my life journey in black and white as I highlighted the fundamentality of moral virtues in society in order to accomplish the set goals in life, which are: faith in God through Jesus; hope; love; perseverance; consistence; and commitment. I wish all these family members God's blessings as they travel their life journeys and remember to urge their own children to do likewise.

ACKNOWLEDGEMENT

I owe gratitude to family ideas for motivating me to write about my life for them and their posterity. Parents are meant to be the first teachers of informal education to their children. They form the foundation for their children's formal education imparted in schools, and provide further spiritual and intellectual enlightenment for their existence in life. I am indebted to my son, Mr Shadreck Banda, for offering himself to type my autobiography and organise the information. I also want to thank my son, Dr Emmanuel Banda, and Kelly Waldrop, who took pains to read through my narrative and edit it. The team spirit experienced in putting ideas to be meaningfully readable is a gain we will forever cherish as a family.

CONTENTS

Introduction 9

CHAPTER ONE

Autobiography of Rev J.C Banda 13

My Quest for Upper Primary School Education 17

CHAPTER TWO

My Secondary School Education 21

Teacher Trainees' Graduation 23

CHAPTER THREE

Passion to be a Minister of Religion 27

A Vivid Call to be a Minister of Religion 29

God's Unfolding Plan for my Service
as an Ordained Minister 42

My Mission to Fulfil According to the
Lord's Great Commission 44

CHAPTER FOUR

Children's Education 53

Rev. Josephat Chaponda Banda as a Married Man 54

Mrs Mavis Banda's Education and Experience 56

Rev. J.C. Banda and Mrs M Banda's Children's Education 57

Experience During my Retirement so Far 61

Praying Ceaselessly - a Christian Helpful Practice 62

Christian Virtues for Morality 64

INTRODUCTION

It is said, "There is no smoke without fire." It was the author's passion to share his experiences that led him to write his autobiography so that people of all ages and backgrounds could glean some invaluable insights and lessons from them. People are like written books that should be read. Some of these books are so educative and instructive that they enhance knowledge in one's sphere of educational or professional life, whereas some are informative to heighten the level of consciousness or enlighten the readers about life in general. Others are fictions, comedies, and tragedies for entertainment. All of these serve the different purposes for which they are written.

This autobiographical narrative serves to help the young and old alike to understand that there is light at the end of the tunnel. Life is a journey with a beginning and an end. In travelling these life journeys, there are hoops to jump over, sharp bends to negotiate, and slippery, rough, bumpy, smooth, dark, and light parts that demand the traveller be cautious and resilient to achieve one's set goals or plans. Courage, persistence, diligence, honesty, determination, and perseverance are some of the indispensable and cardinal principles or virtues required to accomplish one's aims in life.

Teaching the importance of knowing our origins and keeping genealogies for the sake of posterity provided another impetus for this autobiography. With his Christian background, the author ardently believes that God is the Creator of the universe. He created all animate and inanimate things on earth. Human beings, homo sapiens, are endowed with souls and minds that are superior to those of other creatures in the animal group. They are social and religious beings created in the image of God. They know that there is a God, although some profess a diametrically contrary view about His existence. This knowledge makes them religiously inclined to develop different beliefs about God for whom they live to worship, glorify, and elevate above all other humanly instituted authorities. With such an esoteric understanding of God, believers hold that the God they worship is the God of history. Since God is an integral part of the history we make, He influences people spiritually, mentally, and physically through His general revelation. Science, philosophy, and different religions impact human attitudes and behaviour. Hence, human beings living in such a pluralistic world do not always agree on all moral principles as they co-exist. Yet, God is manifestly involved in our lives to guide and protect us and not detached from events happening around us. When we die, our bodies may remain in the graves but the souls return to the Creator. Christianity teaches that the dead will, one day, be resurrected, the departed souls will return to the dead bodies, and the whole human being – body, soul and mind – will be transformed into a celestial body similar to that of Jesus when He was resurrected from the dead. Those who will be justified by God on Judgement Day will live with God eternally, but those who will be condemned will perish forever.

As we nurture children in the world in which we live, societal norms and values synergistically come into play for the development of self-control, resilience, tolerance, adaptation, selflessness, sympathy, and empathy – some of the fundamental and defining characteristics of our humanity. Adults should strive to be responsible and exemplary in their conduct so that they may exercise their authority and influence children to grow into valuable members of society. Adults should help children maintain their cultural identities as they try to navigate the maze of multiculturalism and adapt to the situations in which they find themselves, only assimilating some good and acceptable practices from other cultures. Children need to have the discerning spirit to choose what is right from what is against their faith or culture to avoid inciting the anger of God, whose spiritual and moral standards are sacrosanct.

By Rev. Josephat Chaponda Banda
BA (Hons) UZ; B.Th. (UNISA);
Dip. in Theol.; Cert. in Ed.

CHAPTER ONE

Autobiography of Rev J. C. Banda

My father, Alexander Chaponda Banda, son of Kafanini Banda and Mudankhanya Limbani Banda, was born in Nguluwe Village under the authority of Chief Mshawa of the Ngoni tribe. My mother, Adesi Daka Banda, was born in Kamukuwe Village. Both villages are in the Eastern Province of Zambia in Chipata and are under the paramount authority of Chief Mpezeni of the Ngoni tribe of the Zulu origin.

My father, who was adventurous, walked from Fort Jameson – a city in Zambia that is now known as Chipata – through the western part of Mozambique to reach Bindura in Southern Rhodesia (now Zimbabwe), to seek employment. He proceeded to Mazoe Citrus Estate where he worked as a farm labourer. Six years later, he invited my mother, who had remained in Fort Jameson, to join him. She travelled by bus from Chipata to Lusaka and then by train from Lusaka to Salisbury, which is now known as Harare, Zimbabwe's capital city. From there she travelled by train to Bindura, where she was warmly welcomed by my father. They then travelled together from Bindura to Glendale by train, before walking to reach the Mazoe Citrus Estate compound.

My four brothers – Simeon, Everson, Shadreck, and Benson – and my sister, Dinah, were born while my parents lived and worked at the Mazoe Citrus Estate. Later on, my parents moved to Bindura, where my father was employed as a mine labourer. My brother Habakkuk and I, the last born of their children, were born at Kimberley Gold Mine about four miles east of the town of Bindura. I was born on the 14th of May 1941 and was baptized Jehoshaphat in the same year in October by Rev. J.J. Jackson of the Church of Central Africa Presbyterian (CCAP).

After working at the Kimberley Gold Mine for a long time, my parents decided to move to the Phoenix Prince Mine (now defunct) about three miles west of the town of Bindura. There was no school building in the mine compound, as it was known back then. The compound was just a group of round houses without kitchens that had been built by the mining company. The workers had to build their own kitchens adjacent to the houses out of poles plastered with mud and roofed with grass. The CCAP leaders negotiated with the compound manager to provide a place for the education of the mine workers' children. The church offered the church building to be used as a school, but on Saturdays and Sundays the same building was used for worship.

The church recruited the Headteacher from Malawi, Mr Y. B. Mtima, who in turn recruited teachers from Howard, Bradley Salvation Army schools, and Malawi. All of these teachers, including the Headteacher himself, were untrained but they all had passed what was known as "Standard Six" (the equivalent of Grade Seven), which at the time was considered well-educated enough to teach. Many workers at the mine did not want to send their children to school, especially those from Nyasaland (Malawi), Northern Rhodesia (Zambia), and Portuguese East Africa (Mozambique). My father, however, was very eager to send me to school and enrolled me into "Sub A," which is now called Grade One. I developed a very keen interest in learning, but towards the end of my Sub A year I was annoyed by my class teacher, whom I thought acted unfairly by hitting me on the head with the side of a blackboard ruler. The teacher had asked the class to close their eyes to pray. I closed mine, but when he said, "Amen!" I opened my eyes. One of the pupils in the class reported that "a certain pupil" had not closed his eyes when the teacher was praying, which meant, of course, that he was also a culprit. The teacher then decided to hit us all on our heads with the side of a ruler for good measure. I became so angry that I took my slate on which I practised writing and left the classroom. That incident robbed me of all of my enthusiasm for learning, and I refused to be persuaded to go back to school by my parents that year. I found out that most of my friends had made significant strides in their education and were able to write words on the ground and sing songs in English and the Bantu language of Chinyanja, also known as Chichewa. Furthermore, I missed my friends when I stayed at home, and I was lonely and could not stand idle for so long. So, the following year, my parents had their way and I found myself back in the classroom again.

When I returned to school, I was more eager to learn than ever before. I was greatly motivated in Standards Two and Three. When I was in Standard Three, my teacher, who was the Headteacher – Mr Y.B. Mtima – would ask for my help in teaching the women who took the Adult Education class in the afternoon. His wife used to bring him food at school, and it caused me great discomfort to eat with our Headteacher, dipping morsels of thick maize flour porridge called sadza (Shona) or nsima (Chinyanja/Chichewa) in the same plate of relish. According to our cultural dictates, it was an oddity for a boy of my age to dip in the same plate with an elder. Mr Mtima was interested in singing and forming choirs for competitions in Bindura, Mazoe Citrus Estate, Harare, and Bulawayo. I was in the school choir and was chosen to represent our Phoenix Prince Mine School in reciting Revelation 21: 1-5. Since he could not pronounce some of the words, the European compound manager asked Mr Mtima to let me practise reciting the text in his office under his supervision, twice per week, in preparation for the competition at the Stodard Hall in Mbare, Harare. I came first in the competition, which was adjudicated by Rev. Garfield Todd, who was then Prime Minister of Southern Rhodesia. I was given a big Bible with shiny golden sides. We also went to Bulawayo as a school choir, and we did well. The competition was held in the Hindo Hall and we used to eat at 'Emunhambetini' Eating House. Travelling by train to Harare and Bulawayo was an enjoyable treat for us all.

I completed Standard Three at the top of my class but could not secure a place in Howard Primary School or Bradley Primary School, the two nearby boarding schools. Our Headteacher, Mr Mtima, told us that the new CCAP boarding school was going to open its doors for students specifically from CCAP schools in 1955, but that did not happen then. Sadly, my whole class from P.P. Mine School had to repeat Standard Three because no teacher was found to teach Standard Four. Some of my classmates decided to seek employment at the mine. At the time I was repeating the class, my father had severed ties with the CCAP. He had started to organise those who used to worship in the Dutch Reformed Church in Northern Rhodesia (Zambia) to come together and worship on their own under a tree. When some of the worshippers in the CCAP followed my father in this endeavour, those loyal to the CCAP reported my father to the compound manager for "causing disharmony" in the compound.

My father was summoned by the compound manager to his office. Since my father had very little education, he was assisted by an interpreter. The compound manager found my father innocent because he was also a Dutch Reformed Church member, and understood my father's desire to worship as he did back home.

The manager was pleased to hear that my father was a fellow member of the Dutch Reformed Church and contacted Rev. J. P. Reluex, who was residing in Waterfalls, to see if he could assist this new group of worshippers of the Dutch Reformed Church. Rev. Reluex, whose church centre was Morgenster Mission in Fort Victoria, now known as Masvingo, visited the new congregation at the mine.

My Quest for Upper Primary School Education

My father moved forward with establishing the new congregation by planning to build a church building. My eldest brother, Simeon, was a builder in Mt Darwin and came to my father's aid by building the church at the mine. Church members roofed the building with grass because they could not afford to buy the sturdy corrugated iron sheets that were needed. Still, with their new building complete, the church membership kept growing in leaps and bounds. My father also had the opportunity to talk to Rev. Reluex about my plight. I was repeating Standard Three, and I wanted to go on to Standard Four. Rev. Reluex talked to the Principal of Morgenster Mission, Mr Brand, who was pleased to see my impeccable and meritorious Standard Three school results. Without any misgivings or reservations, I was offered a place for Standard Four at Morgenster Mission. Morgenster Mission, situated near the Great Zimbabwe Ruins, was founded in Fort Victoria (Masvingo) in Zimbabwe on 9th September 1891 by the Rev. A.A. Louw Senior. This Christian institution had, and still has, great influence in Zimbabwe generally, and especially among the Karanga people. Its motto is written in Latin, "Deus Saxum Meum," meaning God is my rock. It has a monument of a candle near the Printing Press, representing the morning star from which the name of the school is derived. "Morgen" (or "morning") and "star" join together to form the name Morgenster, which translates to Nyamasase in Shona.

When schools were about to open for the year, Rev. Reluex sent a word to my father to meet him in Harare so that he could show me where to board the Rhodesia Railways mail and passenger bus to Fort Victoria (Masvingo). We travelled from Bindura to Harare to meet with Rev. Reluex, who directed me to Morgenster Mission. I boarded the bus to Fort Victoria Railway station and then walked some one hundred and fifty yards to board another bus that took me to Morgenster Mission. Arriving at Morgenster Mission to further my studies was a surreal experience. I never dreamt of advancing my education beyond Standard Three and I knew at once that this was a golden opportunity for me to assuage my passion for learning. In Standard Four, I ended the year in class position seven out of forty students because it was my first year to write compositions in the Shona language. I was used to writing compositions in Chinyanja/Chichewa. I had problems with the exercises where we had to fill in the blanks to complete Shona proverbs:

1) Mwana washe ....

2) Chakachenjedza..........................

3) Kure kwegava.............................

4) Muzivi wenzira yeparuware.....................

Instead of leaving the blank spaces unfilled, I guessed words to write, which proved my ignorance. Over time, I learnt some of the proverbs and how to write Shona compositions. I became interested in expressing myself in Shona idioms, like "Madimikira," and in onomatopoeia in Shona, like "Nyaudzosingwi." I soon realised that Shona proverbs were the Shona people's expression of wisdom in their culture. As students, we also sharpened our intellectual acumen by identifying the meanings of riddles.

In the upper primary school (Standard Four to Standard Six), I was very good at English because my mother had bought me a Michael West English Dictionary. That Dictionary included idioms that I mastered and frequently used in my English expressions. I also learnt the meaning of words that I found in simple literature books and newspapers like The Recorder and The Rhodesia Herald. When I was in Standard Five and Six, I became adept at ordering books from South Africa, like the Student's Companion, which had similes, diminutive case words, opposite words, word formation using prefixes and suffixes, and more. Another book I ordered was called Phrase and Idiom. When the parcels of books reached our school, the Boarding Master or a school captain or prefect would call out the names of those who had received packages during meals in the dining hall. It felt good to hear my parcels called out in front of the other students.

I was also very good at Arithmetic, Nature Study, History, Geography, Hygiene, and Scripture (Bible Knowledge). I continued to work arduously and assiduously in my Shona lessons and kept improving in my drive to learn. In Standard Five my class teacher, Mr Richard Takavarasha, was proud of my ability in writing English compositions and grammar. I kept my English and Grammar exercise books that contained motivating comments written by class teachers. I even showed them to my students when I was a teacher at Makosa Primary School to motivate them in composition writing.

I had responsibility thrust upon me in Standard Five when the teaching staff chose me to be one of the school prefects to help teachers and the Boarding Master, Mr Boniface Bwatikona

Charumbira, to maintain order and discipline at school. Students were expected to strictly adhere to rules and observe social etiquette at all times, especially in the dining hall and during evening study hours. As a co-educational institution, we used to have evening studies with boys and girls mixed together. When the evening studies were over, prefects took turns walking the girls safely back to their dormitories, which were about 400 metres away from the classrooms. When the girls were safe in the hands of their matron, it was mission accomplished for the prefects.

Prefects had some notebooks in which they wrote down the names of recalcitrant students and submitted the list to the Boarding Master. Come Saturday afternoon, the mischievous students were punished by doing all sorts of manual work around the school. Prefects were urged to be well-disciplined themselves so they would maintain the authority and respect needed to discipline others. On Sundays, students had to march to church in single file, and it was the duty of prefects to ensure that orderliness was maintained. In Standard Six, I had the privilege to be under the tutelage of Mr H. O. B. Zimuto, who was also the Headmaster of Morgenster Primary School. I admired my Headmaster's English diction and accent when he was teaching. He was softly spoken but a strict disciplinarian. When I completed Standard Six, Mr Zimuto facilitated my application for a Form One place at Hartzell High School or Old Mutare Mission.

CHAPTER TWO

My Secondary School Education

At Hartzell High School, when I was in Form One, I was chosen by my English teacher, Miss Smock, to perform in a play after reading some passages from the Gilbert and Sullivan musical, "The King and I" or "Anna and the King of Siam." Siam is the former name of the country now known as Thailand in Asia. I was chosen to act as the King of Siam in the play, and Miss Margaret Munangatire, my classmate, was chosen to be my main wife, with several fellow female students acting as my minor wives. Miss Margaret Munangatire and I were the main characters in the play that took us three hours on the stage, accompanied by singing and dancing. Rev. Marcia Ball, a missionary from the United States of America who taught at the school, was the pianist. Some European spectators were invited from Mutare to witness the show staged by the Form 1 actors and actresses in the Beit Hall at the Old Mutare Mission. We performed very well to the satisfaction of the spectators. From that time, I found myself in the spotlight, and the children of the missionaries at Old Mutare used to call me "King of Siam" whenever we met in the school grounds. My exuberant performance in the drama also garnered for me the attention and admiration of teachers and missionaries at the school.

While in the first year of secondary education, my school held a prize-giving day in the Beit Hall for students who excelled in academic and extracurricular activities across the school. I was awarded a book prize in drama. This drama, in my view, inadvertently opened a way for me to be awarded a scholarship for both my secondary school education and teacher's training at the Old Mutare Mission. My parents were no longer able to pay my school fees as they were preparing to retire and go back home to Northern Rhodesia (Zambia). My father had worked at the Phoenix Prince Gold Mine without any pension for thirteen years. The little money he had saved was just enough to enable my parents to return home. Once in Zambia, they settled in Kankhoma Village, under Chief Mafuta, at a family farm that was provided by the government for settlement. My parents passed on to eternal glory as devout members of the Dutch Reformed Church. I was so fortunate that the staff at Old Mutare Mission met me at my point of need and decided to pay my tuition fees until I completed my teacher's training at the same place.

Working for Pocket Money During School Holidays

I had not grown up in privilege and plenty, but with my parents retired and my school being paid for by a scholarship, the grim reality of a life of struggle and deprivation stared me right in the face. I could not continue to live on the generosity of my teachers and missionaries at the school for everything that I needed, and I quickly realised that I needed to toil and fend for myself to augment whatever little came my way. During the school holidays, when others went home to be with their families, I stayed behind to work for pocket money to buy the essentials that I needed to keep me afloat when school was in session. I painted teachers' houses and also the classrooms at the primary school that was headed by Mr Tauro, who was also the Old Mutare Church choir director. He asked me to paint the primary school toilets as well. Rev. Marcia Ball had me make some flower beds and plant and water the flowers at her office. At times, she asked me to prepare Sunday school materials for Christian Education outreach to rural areas like Chitakatira, Chitenderano, and Nyadire Mission. When my parents left Rhodesia (Zimbabwe) for Northern Rhodesia (Zambia), I did not expect that any financial assistance would come from them. My brother, who was working at The Rhodesia Herald, had a big family to care for, and it dawned on me that I had no other option but to work hard to achieve my educational goal.

Teacher Trainees' Graduation

Graduation Day! Graduation Day! In the year 1962, in Ehnes Memorial United Methodist Church, a very exciting event took place that made many teacher training graduates shed tears of joy. This was the most interesting day in my twenty-one years of life, and it felt like a day of liberation from hard work to be on my own without depending heavily on my well-wishers who sacrificed their financial and other resources for me to acquire the much-needed education. The school choir, conducted by Mr Tauro, a great singer, sang a song with the lyrics, "There is coming a day to rest a while when we lay our burdens down." This graduation opened the door for us to be authentically recognised as fully qualified teachers, equipped with the knowledge, skills, and dispositions to go out into the field to execute our professionalism with confidence and transform lives and our society through education.

We were going to earn money to support ourselves, family members, and others in need. On that graduation day, I was recruited by a white missionary schools' manager of the United

Methodist Church in Mutoko and Uzumba-Maramba, named Mr Noah. He was stationed at Nyadire Mission. He had driven to the Old Mutare Mission specifically to recruit teachers for  his schools, especially those that were to be elevated from lower primary schools, from Sub A to Standard Three, like Manhemba, Chitekwe, Bondamakara, Kawere and Makosa to mention a few. I was recruited to open a Standard Five class at Makosa Primary School in 1963, and that's where I cut my professional teeth. I was very excited to have my own class where I could demonstrate my professional expertise. I greatly enjoyed the respect I was given by the fellow staff members, the students, and the parents of the pupils. I took my Standard Five class to Standard Six, where most of my pupils did well in Arithmetic and English Language and qualified for secondary school education at different schools. I really enjoyed teaching because it offered me the rare opportunity to shape the lives of young people so they could become informed, active, engaged, conscientious, and productive members of society. There was no greater joy and pride for me as a teacher than seeing my students taking their place in society and occupying positions of influence and leadership in various spheres of life.

At this school, I was a young man of 21 years old, and turned 22 in May of the same year when I started to teach as a qualified teacher. I was asked to be a teaching Deputy Headteacher to Mr Zechariah Nyerenyere. After teaching for a couple of years, I became the headmaster of the school from 1965 to 1966.

In 1967, I was appointed the Headmaster of Chikwizo Mission of the United Methodist Church in Mutoko, and I remained in that position until 1970. It was then that I was appointed the Headmaster of Katsukunya Primary School of the United Methodist Church in Mutoko. I stayed in that school until 1973.

These schools were all in rural areas where people had mixed feelings towards schools and the teaching staff. At Makosa, some of the villagers tried to interfere with the pupils' extracurricular activities and evening social activities. They were met with my fury if their behaviour was unbecoming. Those who came to witness the pupils' activities had to observe the rules and expectations as the pupils did in school. In most cases, the pupils were respectful and very willing to learn, which made teaching enjoyable.

CHAPTER THREE

Passion to be a Minister of Religion

Although I served as a teacher and Headmaster at various schools in the Mutoko District, including Makosa, Chikwizo and Katsukunya primary schools, I felt an abiding passion to become a Minister of Religion. When I was in the primary school at Morgenster Mission (1956 - 1958), my father used to encourage me to preach in the church at Bindura and Glendale during the school holidays. He had a strong and instinctive feeling that Morgenster Mission was the most auspicious environment to nurture my religious inclinations so that I could become a Minister of Religion one day. I used to be very attentive when great and charismatic preachers like Rev. Dr Van der Merwe, Rev. S. K. Jackson, and Rev. Bimha preached fluently and powerfully. They became my role models whom I emulated. My father had a great vision for my future and wanted me to go to South Africa to learn how to speak Afrikaans like the white Dutch Reformed Ministers did. Much to his displeasure, things never turned out the way he had hoped.

I used to write short sermons in my notebooks, getting some sermon illustrations from a booklet written by Rev. S. K. Jackson. Rev. Jackson was one of our ministers and the writer of the Shona grammar book, which was used in some of the secondary schools.

I developed an intense interest in preaching and used to practise here and there when the opportunity presented itself. My father was very inspirational and instrumental in my vocational calling to be a Minister of Religion. However, each time I witnessed the way Ministers of Religion were disparaged and denigrated by some of the people whom they led and shepherded, it made me hot under the collar. I vividly remember an incident that happened during a charge conference when Rev. N. Madzinga was the District Superintendent of Mutoko District and I was the Headmaster of Chikwizo Mission. There at Chikwizo, my wife, Mavis Banda, became a full member of the Ruwadzano RweWadzimai (RRW – Women's Organisation), and I also became a full member of a group known as Vabvuwi weUnited Methodist Church – a fisher of men of the United Methodist Church. The finance committee used to write on the blackboard how much they had paid the pastor and how much they owed him in stipends or wages. Pastors used to be paid quarterly and yet they were in short supply of food and money to send their children to school. Being a Minister of Religion meant being prepared to live on a measly wage and, at times, being at the mercy of those people you shepherded.

Despite what I witnessed and heard about the abhorrent manner in which pastors were treated, I had a burning desire to be a preacher. To wet my feet in my newly found passion, I started off as a local preacher at Chikwizo Mission in Mutoko. I thought this steppingstone would assuage my desire to become a fully-fledged pastor one day. Sadly, I found myself succumbing to the lures of the teaching profession. I liked teaching and enjoyed the prospects of being promoted to the position of Headmaster wherever I taught, so I continued in that profession for several more years, until 1973. No matter how much I liked teaching, the nagging and lingering desire to be a preacher caused me sleepless nights. I got tired of running away from God, and I decided to give in.

A Vivid Call to be a Minister of Religion

In 1973, during my time as the Headmaster of Katsukunya Primary School, the RRW Women's Revival was held at the Nyadire Camp Ground of the United Methodist Church near Nyadire River. My wife and I went there to worship with others. There I was cornered by the word of God preached by our great preacher, Bishop Abel Tendekayi Muzorewa. He preached about Jonah who was trying to run away from God. Jonah did not go where God wanted him to go for the salvation of the souls of people, but chose to go where the people did not need him as much. I found myself in a similar quandary. My passion was in teaching, and it brought me much joy and a sense of satisfaction to contribute to the holistic development and growth of students. Of course, this was good but God was saying to me that it was not enough. He wanted me to proclaim the gospel and teach His word for the salvation of mankind. Though I was a teacher and I could teach and preach as a layperson, God knew me much better than I knew myself. At this Women's Revival, I surrendered myself to God and remembered the United Methodist Church hymn, "Itai Mponesi izvo munoda," "Have Thine own way Lord."

Our beloved Bishop A.T. Muzorewa preached about Jonah who found it very difficult to preach the message of repentance to the enemies of his Jewish people, the Assyrians, who enslaved and shattered the ten tribes of the Northern Kingdom of Israel. It is always wise to go where we are sent, because He sends us for a purpose in the grand scheme of His works. God knows all things and human situations much more than we do. There are times where some people in their lamentable ignorance act as if they know things or situations better than God to their detriment or peril.

As the Bishop was reaching the climax of his sermon, he asked the congregants whether we had experienced a time when we had encountered God. He wanted to know whether God had asked us to carry out His mission and we had resisted because we had our own plans and goals. Worshipping God entails sacrifices or suffering for God and the people to please God Himself. We should learn to be humble in order to be good followers of Jesus, who was humble to the extent of dying on the cross vicariously for the sins of mankind. I was moved by the bishop's sermon. He invited the congregants to pray silently for a while, and after a time, he shouted, "Amen!" and asked if anyone wanted to share testimonies of their personal encounter with God when they were praying. A number of people stood up to testify briefly, including me. God wanted me to go where I was not yet ready to go. His will but not my will had to be done. I aired my views that I had been behaving like Jonah for many years, but God was patient with me. Teaching people in schools was not bad, but He wanted me to do something else that was not much different from teaching in the classroom. I had made up my mind to resign from teaching and go to a theological school to train as a Minister of Religion of the United Methodist Church.

Since I was a local preacher and a fisher of man "Mubvuwi," it was easy for people to approve me as a ministerial candidate at the local church administrative board meeting and Circuit or Charge levels. My pastor at that time was Rev. Philemon Gurupira. My name was sent to the chairperson of the Conference Board of Ordained Ministry, who was Rev. Samuel Munjoma. The interviews were held in the town of Rusape. Mr Jairos Wirikidzayi Mafondokoto (now Reverend Mafondokoto) and I were successful candidates for ministerial training. In contrast to Mr Mafondokoto, who was single, I was a married man with five children when I made this life-changing decision to quit teaching and train as a pastor. I resigned from teaching after having taught for eleven years. When I was making some preparations to go to Epworth Theological College, now the United Theological College in Epworth, Hatfield, Zimbabwe, I was told that the United Methodist Church had no funds for my college tuition. I was devastated by this decision to renege on their earlier promise to offer me financial assistance because I had already resigned from my job. God had a plan for my life, and I had surrendered to His will. If God has chosen you for his divine purposes, He removes obstacles and barriers that come your way. I notified Rev. Marcia Ball, who had assisted me financially when I was in high school and teachers' training college, about my plight. She was both stunned and worried about this sudden twist of fate. Fortunately, one day, Rev. Ball received a phone call from a retired American missionary, Ms Edna Elliot, who was working in Japan and had visited Zimbabwe. She called to ask where the United Methodists gathered for church services on Sundays. During the call, Rev. Ball made mention of my struggles to Ms Elliot, and they agreed to talk about the matter at Hunyani. They met on Sunday and worshipped together there. After the church service, they talked about my predicament.

Ms Elliot inquired about the cost of tuition and other fees for my ministerial training at Epworth Theological College and was told that it was within the ballpark of $1,000 per year. Without any disinclination, she generously wrote a cheque for $4,000 to cover my four years of training at the college. Rev. Ball quickly got in touch with me to break the good news and to urge me to expedite my preparations to go to Epworth Theological College. I was truly grateful to Ms Elliot for her extreme generosity and kindness that had translated my dream of becoming a Minister of Religion into reality.

However, when everything appeared to be going swimmingly well, another obstacle reared its ugly face. When I was in my first year at the college, I got the surprise of my life when Rev. J. W. Mafondokoto and I were asked to pay additional money towards our fees, even though the fees had been paid in full. We approached Rev. Erickson and Rev. Dr Maurice Culver, our lecturers, to express our lack of wherewithal to pay the additional fees. They resolved that, instead of a one-time lump sum payment, we could pay in instalments until the additional fees were paid in full. We had no other choice but to pay from the meagre allowances we received from the college over the year. Raising fees for students who were already enrolled and had paid in full was unprecedented and never experienced again after us at the college. Nevertheless, we remained undeterred, resolute, and unswerving in our desire to train as Ministers of Religion and continued to learn with revitalised zeal and enthusiasm to overcome any barriers we encountered. I was mostly driven by the strong conviction that what was meant to be would always find its way. I believed that I was set apart for an important task and that the one who chose me for this mission would see me through all the roadblocks set before me.

When I was in the second year of training, Rev. Dr Maurice Culver, our lecturer in Homiletics, advised me to embark on university studies with the University of South Africa (UNISA) concurrently with reading for my Diploma in Theology. Our lecturer, Rev. Dr Chrispen G. Mazobere, and others opted to help me and three other students study for a Bachelor of Theology degree (B.Th.). The printed modules from UNISA were quite handy and provided us with the lectures and textbooks to be studied. We wrote our assignments and posted them to be marked by our lecturers and professors at the University of South Africa. In addition to studying Systematic Theology and Theological Ethics as my major subjects, I also studied Practical Theology, Science of Religion and Missiology, the Old Testament, the New Testament and Church History, just to mention a few. Embarking on undergraduate studies concurrently with my Diploma in Theology was no mean feat, and it called for striking a delicate and reasonable balance among multiple imperatives and responsibilities vying for my time and attention. Ms Elliot, who had then gone back to Pittsburgh, Pennsylvania in the USA, paid the additional fees that were needed for me to undertake my university work. She also bought me a big single Interpreter's Bible commentary for all of the books in the Bible.

I never got to meet Ms Edna Elliot, and all my efforts to even get hold of her photograph from America hit a snag. She was God-sent, and it was my heart's desire to meet her in person and thank her for her enormous and selfless contribution in helping me realise my academic and vocational dreams. She only told me to thank God for everything she did for me. This was very touching to me even to this day. I saw Jesus in Edna Elliot, who was out of sight to me and yet real and existing in agape love. I'm eternally grateful to her for transforming my life and teaching me the true essence of selfless giving in making a difference in other people's lives, and for being the silver lining to many of the most despairing moments in my life journey. I am who I am today because someone cared, someone identified a need and reached out in love and compassion to meet that need.

At Epworth Theological College (1974-1977), I enjoyed my studies and sought out opportunities for my holistic growth and development. The late Bishop Christopher Jokomo was in the third year when I was a freshman at the college. During my four-year stint as a student there, the college was made up of the following denominations: The Methodist Church in Zimbabwe; United Methodist Church; United Church of Christ; Anglican Church; United Congregational Church of Southern Africa; Presbyterian Church; and Zionist Church. After graduating with a Diploma in Theology (Epworth Theological College), I later completed my B.Th. (Bachelor of Theology) with the University of South Africa while working as a student chaplain and teacher at Murewa Mission. I also acquired a B.A (Hons) with the University of Zimbabwe. It was a long and arduous professional and academic journey that started with the acquisition of a Certificate in Education (Hartzell Teacher's College, Mutare).

Short History of My Service in the United Methodist Church

1974 – 1977: Student Pastor at Epworth Theological College Hatfield, Harare, Zimbabwe. At this interdenominational theological college, my fellow student pastors elected me to be President of the Students Union for two consecutive years (1976 and 1977). I represented the students at the College Council Meetings and aired some requests for their welfare to the Principal.

1978 – 1980: Appointed by Bishop Abel Muzorewa to be an Associate Pastor to Rev. Patrick Nyamukapa, student chaplain and Murewa High School teacher.

1979: Appointed the Deputy Headmaster to Mr Samson Nyamugama at Murewa High School. During that time, it was very difficult to maintain school discipline, as some of the students were inclined to cause trouble for teachers whom they knew were in the midst of a significant dilemma. Freedom fighters were sending messengers to Murewa High School searching for financial assistance. We took up collections to help the freedom fighters, but we tried hard to keep this practice as secret as we could because, if we had been discovered, we would be punished heavily by the regime of that time.

1981 – 1988: Appointed by Bishop Abel Muzorewa to reopen Nyamuzuwe High School, which had been destroyed during the time of the protracted war of liberation in Zimbabwe. The roofs of some of the teachers' houses had been vandalised, a three-classroom block where school furniture had been stored for safety had been burnt down, and boarding equipment had been stolen by villagers. The laboratory equipment was vandalised and so was the library. The generator for electricity was destroyed, and Nyamuzuwe High School had been closed down for three years. I was appointed to reopen the school to be a functional High School once more. The pioneers of the school after it reopened were a mixed bag of traditional and non-traditional school-going age groups. These students did not have the luxury of laying on beds but spent the greater part of the year spreading their blankets on the floor. During weekends, we mobilised students to go out into the community to ask for beds and other school furniture that villagers had helped themselves to without permission. This repossession venture was made easier by the fact that some of the students belonged to those communities and knew exactly which households had helped themselves to the school property. Most community members were very cooperative because they knew that the ultimate beneficiaries were their children, and they also did not want to live with the stigma of having stolen school property. High on my priority list was the construction of two new classroom blocks and a science laboratory, and repairing some of the teachers' houses to make them habitable.

Reopening Nyamuzuwe high school was no mean feat. Some who had been approached for the task before me found it insurmountable and highly risky given the prevailing political climate soon after the liberation war. I enrolled three streams of Form One pupils in 1981 and recruited teachers, a boarding master (Mr Diba Marere), a matron (Mrs Njagu), an administrative secretary, and a bursar. Among the first staff members to be recruited were Mr Daniel Makawa, Dr Mildred Taylor (a missionary from the USA), Mr Masunda (now a medical practitioner), and Mr Victor Madzinga.

The first typewriter that was used in my office and the duplicating machine had been hidden in the sand near a stream. I was shown this place by one of my church members, a fellow member of Fisher of Men UMC, Mr Chajamai. We unearthed this office equipment for immediate use.

The church at Nyamuzuwe Mission had not been in use for the three years since the school had closed down. The church building was used by villagers as a storeroom for community relief food. I decided to approach the leaders in the community to have the relief food removed from the church building, since the President of the country had sanctioned the reopening of the mission centre. They wondered where else the food could be stored. We approached Mr Kanyuchi, a friendly businessman who owned buses and shops, to assist us by storing the relief food in his storeroom behind his shop at Nyamuzuwe Township. My wife, three of our children, and I swept and scrubbed the church floor in readiness for the opening day of the school. The local church members were afraid to go to church at that time because it was politically dangerous to be associated with the United Methodist Church, whose Bishop was the then-Prime Minister of the short-lived Zimbabwe-Rhodesia and was labelled a traitor of the liberation struggle.

So many things had to be put in place before the opening day. We had no vehicle to ferry foodstuffs from the Mutoko business centre. At times we used Dr Taylor's small VW car, which had a trunk in the front of the car. When we managed to secure a generator for electricity, we needed a bigger vehicle urgently. The boarding school constantly needed supplies from Mutoko and Harare to keep it operating smoothly. Confronted with the hassle of transport, I had to dig into my pocket and decided to buy a personal 404 yellow Peugeot station wagon. I used my family car to ferry diesel from Mutoko business centre to Nyamuzuwe Mission. The car worked for a year or so, after which we got a shot in the arm from the responsible authority of the school, the United Methodist Church. The Church bought us a Land Rover and a new generator to replace the old one that I had bought from Kamoto Farm, near Nyadire Mission, where we used to buy vegetables for the boarders.

Opening the church's doors to the six local churches around Nyamuzuwe Mission proved to be a daunting task. Church members were fearful of coming into the open and identifying themselves as United Methodist members. Being a United Methodist church member during that perilous transitional period from war to independence was synonymous with being a supporter of Bishop Muzorewa's political party. Church members chose to remain in the shadows for their own safety and security, and I had to devise ways to reach out to them. I was told the names of some of our members, and I managed to convince a few to come to church. I explained how the newly elected Prime Minister of Zimbabwe had sanctioned the reopening of all schools that were closed due to the war and that communities were being urged to support such endeavours. We spread the word of God to the local churches, and some students were actively involved in church revivals. The Nyamuzuwe Circuit of congregations started to function gradually. Rev. Alan M. Gurupira was appointed to teach at Nyamuzuwe High School and to serve as a student chaplain. He also served in Nyamuzuwe Circuit as an associate pastor and contributed immensely in stabilising the circuit. The political leaders were a bit hard on me. From time to time, I was called to political meetings at Nyamuzuwe Township for questioning on trumped up charges. At last, political leaders from Marondera came to my rescue when they warned the vocal village political leaders against their attitudes and behaviour directed towards me and the school on political grounds.

In 1989, after an eight-year stint at the helm of Nyamuzuwe High School, I was appointed to be the District Superintendent of the Murewa District. I was glad to come back to the same place I served as a teacher and Deputy Headmaster but in a new capacity. As District Superintendent, I supervised circuits in Murewa and Uzumba Maramba Pfungwe, as well as the Malawi mission area. During my time in the Murewa District, I was privileged to accompany a high-levelled delegation led by Bishop Muzorewa that included Mr John Zvinoera and other church leaders. We travelled to Lilongwe by bus through Nyamapanda and Tete in Mozambique. The purpose of the visit was to see if the then-President of Malawi, Dr Hastings Kamuzu Banda, would allow us to establish the United Methodist Church in Malawi. The trip was very successful.

When I left Nyamuzuwe to serve as District Superintendent, my 404 Peugeot succumbed to the rough dusty roads and broke down. I took it to Harare for repairs, but the astronomical amount of money required to get it back on the road left me with no other option but to sell it. I found myself in yet another quandary – getting to all those circuits under my jurisdiction with no car. I had to rely heavily on the personal vehicle of the then-District lay leader, Mr Enock Nyamupanda. I only served in the district for one year before being appointed a lecturer at the United Theological College.

1990 - 1996

From 1990 to 1993, I taught Ethics, Church History, Christian Education, and Sociology of Religion at the United Theological  College where I was a student from 1974 to 1977.

I was then appointed the Principal of the United Theological College from 1994 to 1996. I also lectured in Philosophical Ethics, Christian Ethics, Christian Education, and Worship. During the same time, I was appointed pastor-in-charge of the Hatfield United Methodist circuit. During my time as the

Rev. J.C. BANDA (PRINCIPAL) 1994

Principal of the college, I found that the female student pastors experienced a shortage of accommodation, so I organised a hostel to be constructed at the college.

1997 - 2004

I was appointed the first District Superintendent of Masvingo District, and then in 2004, I was appointed the Superintendent of two districts – the Masvingo District and the Bulawayo-Midlands District that covered Kwekwe, Gweru, Bulawayo, Hwange, Victoria Falls, and Botswana. The United Methodist Church was a newcomer in Masvingo, where the Roman Catholic Church and the African Reformed Church were the old and dominant churches. During my time as Superintendent there, the Masvingo Circuit managed to source funds from the General Board of Global Ministries in the USA and bought the Masvingo Inner City Sanctuary. The Masvingo District was once part of the Bulawayo-Midlands District before its inception in 1997. When I was appointed to superintend over two districts, the head office for the two districts was located in Gweru. Travelling was very extensive and at times the laity with whom I travelled would offer to relieve me by driving.

2005

When my tenure as District Superintendent for the two districts was over, Bishop Nhiwatiwa appointed me an associate Pastor at Revelation United Methodist Church along Lomagundi Road in Mabelreign, Harare, from January to the 5th of February 2005. After my very brief stint at Revelation UMC, the Bishop appointed me to serve brothers and sisters in Christ in diaspora. I left Zimbabwe with my wife and our last-born son for the United Kingdom and touched down at Gatwick International Airport on the 7th of February 2005. My appointment was to serve in the North Charge of the United Methodist Church, which encompassed Birmingham, Coventry, Wolverhampton, and Manchester. When the Charge grew bigger to include Sheffield, Leeds, Crewe, and Bristol, it was divided into the North Charge and the Midlands Charge. I remained serving in the Midlands Charge from 2010 to 31st March 2020. Dividing the North Charge into two charges was intended to support the rapid growth of the United Methodist Church in the United Kingdom, but it left the North Charge unable to support an ordained Minister on its own. On the other hand, the distance to be covered by the pastor was reduced remarkably to a much more reasonable area. For the North Charge to be viable, it needed to gain numerical strength through evangelism or restructuring involving the nearby Charges.

2015 - 2018

The Bishop appointed me as acting District Superintendent for the Mission areas in diaspora (the UK, Republic of Ireland, Canada, Australia, and New Zealand). The shortage of ordained Pastors and the distances to be covered by the District Superintendent, who was also a Pastor-in-Charge, made this role very hard. With God's help one could only do one's best, which might be below the mark, leaving the rest to God. The two responsibilities (being Superintendent and Pastor) need to be separated in the future for the mutual good of the shepherd and the sheep. Normally, the District Superintendent plays a role in church administration, supervising pastors while helping in planning and motivating the pastors and the parishioners to do better spiritually, morally, and mentally through studying the word of God and worship.

2019 - 2020

I was appointed the Pastor-in-Charge of the Midlands Charge, which is made up of five local churches. Having served as a Minister of Religion for effectively forty-two years, my appointment was to officially end on the 31st March 2020. I now gladly shout, "Ebenezer!"

God is eternally good for me! To abandon my Maker and Saviour would be insanity of the highest magnitude for it's Him who led with through this journey to its final end. Help me God till my departure from the planet!

God's Unfolding Plan for My Service as an Ordained Minister

My ministry in United Methodist Church spans four decades as shown below:

1. Served in the Mrewa District, Mutoko District, Masvingo District, Bulawayo-Midlands District, and Botswana as a teacher, pastor, student chaplain, Headmaster, and District Superintendent.

2. Annually elected Chairman of Pastors' meetings of the Zimbabwe Annual Conference from 1980 - 1989.

3. Lecturer and Principal at United Theological College.

4. Delegate to the meeting for the formation of the United Methodist Church in South Africa.

5. Delegate of the Zimbabwe Annual Conference to Mozambique, Mindolo Zambia, Angola, and the Republic of Congo.

6. Delegate to African Church Growth and Development in Monrovia, Liberia.

7. Accompanied Bishops A. T. Muzorewa, Matthews, and Skeet, in the company of Pastor Mpulula and Pastor Jawati, at different times to have Annual meetings chaired by the bishops and to establish the United Methodist Church in Lilongwe, Malawi.

8. Delegate representing the Zimbabwe United Methodist Conference at a global gathering in Kansas City USA.

9. Delegate to UMC General Conference, 3rd May 2000, Cleveland, Ohio USA.

10. Nominee as one of the three top candidates to be elected as a Bishop for the Zimbabwe Area Episcopal 2004 Elections.

11. Germany holding seminars

12. Propagating the gospel and supervising mission outreach in the UK, Republic of Ireland and Australia.

Though retired from my Church-appointed duties, I remain in service for my Lord, mentally and spiritually, as a traveller homeward. The hymn that should be sung by travellers spiritually is: "Face to Face with Christ my Saviour"

Face to face with Christ my Saviour,
Face to face what will it be,
When with rapture I behold Him,
Jesus Christ who died for me?

Chorus
Face to face shall I behold Him.
Far beyond the starry sky;
Face to face in all His glory, I shall
See Him by and by!

Only faintly now, I see Him,
 with the darkling veil between,
But a blessed day is coming,
When His glory shall be seen.

What rejoicing in His presence,
When are banished grief and pain;
When the crooked ways are straightened,
And the dark things shall be plain.

Face to face! O blissful moment!
Face to face – to see and know;
Face to face with my Redeemer;
Jesus Christ who loves me so.

My Mission to Fulfil According to the Lord's Great Commission

Consequent to my theological training at the Epworth Theological College in Hatfield, Harare, Zimbabwe, I traversed and left footprints in Mrewa, Mtoko, Harare, Masvingo, Midlands, Bulawayo, Hwange, Victoria Falls, and Botswana in fulfilment of the Lord's Great Commission – to preach, teach, and make disciples for Jesus Christ.

When the Zimbabwe Annual Conference decided to evangelise in South Africa, Rev. Isaac Mapipi Mawokomatanda, Mr William Fambayi Marima, and Rev. Samson Mungure pioneered evangelism in this neighbouring country. On one occasion, I joined them on a trip to Gauteng in Johannesburg to meet some

of the Methodist Church members who wanted to join the United Methodist Church. Their leaders included Rev. Mahlatsi and Rev Tobi. We discussed the possibility of accepting them to be members of the United Methodist Church, but they decided to keep on using the Methodist Church uniforms. Some of the young and married church members were presented to be interviewed for theological training at the United Theological

College. We interviewed them, and three of them succeeded. This marked the establishment of the United Methodist Church in South Africa.

As an elected conference delegate to the central conferences, I had the privilege and honour of travelling to the following countries: Mozambique; Angola; Mindolo in Zambia; and Lubumbashi and Kinshasa in the Republic of Congo. I was also elected as a clergy delegate representing the Zimbabwe Annual Conference at the General Conference in Cleveland Ohio, in the USA, in the year 2000. I was chosen as one of the two delegates to attend the United Methodist Church global gathering in Kansas City, USA.

When the Zimbabwe Annual Conference decided to have an outreach in Malawi during the time of Bishop Abel Tendekayi Muzorewa, I was among those who travelled by bus to Lilongwe via the Nyamapanda Road and Mozambique. Bishop A. T. Muzorewa, Rev. Gift Machinga, Mr John Zvinoera and I went to talk to the Malawian pastors who were organising the church in Malawi. I had the unique advantage of being fluent in one of the native languages of Malawi, Chichewa. Upon reading the Book of Discipline of the United Methodist Church, Dr Hastings Kamuzu Banda agreed that the church would be founded in Malawi. The Zimbabwe Annual Conference then started in earnest to establish the church in Lilongwe. The indigenous candidates for ministerial training at the United Theological College were recruited, and after their training, they were urged to go back home to lead the church in Malawi.

When the Zimbabwe Annual Conference found that it would be cost-effective for Malawian theological training students to learn in Malawi, I was among those who went to Mikolongwe Bible College to conduct a feasibility assessment of the theological subjects offered. We were generally satisfied with the curriculum except for one inadequacy. The Bible College in Malawi could not teach the United Methodist Church Polity, its organisational structure, rules, and forms of internal governance. Fortunately for us, Malawian graduates from the United Theological College and those who later furthered their theological education at Africa University in Mutare, came to our rescue. They were asked to teach others about the United Methodist Church Polity in Malawi.

When Bishop Matthews arrived in Zimbabwe as interim Bishop during Bishop Muzorewa's tenure, I was privileged to accompany him to Lilongwe to chair the Mission Area Annual Meeting. This was an occasion for the church in Malawi to give their reports on the various activities and programmes aligned with the overall mission of the United Methodist Church. The church in Malawi was considered a Mission Area approved by the General Conference through which it was funded for its smooth running.

During the time of Bishop Christopher Jokomo, I also accompanied Bishop Skeet (who had come to assist Bishop Jokomo for an interim period) to Malawi. While there he chaired a Mission Area Annual meeting and visited local churches.

In 1984, Mr Nathan Goto and I were sent by the church to Liberia for the Africa Church Growth and Development (ACG&D) Meeting in Monrovia. At this meeting, the Zimbabwe Annual Conference was given its share of the contributions that were made by the American, European, and African United Methodist Churches meant for the growth and development of churches in Africa. Out of that allotment, the Zimbabwe Annual Conference granted the request by the RRW Women's Organisation to fund the purchase of a bus and to start a women's craft shop at the United Methodist Church Head Quarters in Harare.

In 2005, I was appointed by Bishop Nhiwatiwa to serve as a pastor in the United Kingdom. I resided in Birmingham in the North Charge, with eight local churches stretching from Leeds in the north to Bristol in the south, over 200 miles away.

Later on, the charge became too large for one pastor, and it was divided into the North Charge and the Midlands Charge. I then served in the Midlands Charge with five local churches between Crewe and Bristol, a mere 140 miles apart.

In 2011, I served as a voluntary hospital Chaplain at the Black Country NHS Foundation Trust hospital in West Bromwich, Birmingham, during my day off each week. I was awarded the volunteer award the same year by the NHS Foundation Officers in recognition of my service to patients and staff at the hospital.

In 2015, I was appointed to serve as the Pastor of the Midlands Charge and the acting District Superintendent of the Mission Area of the United Methodist Church, which was made up of the United Kingdom, Canada, Australia, and New Zealand. The jurisdiction also extended to the Republic of Ireland.

In 2019, I was appointed to serve as Pastor of the Midlands charge, where I served until the 31st of March 2020, when I officially retired from active ministry. Currently, I reside in Birmingham as a retired minister of the United Methodist Church. This is what the Lord enabled me to do in His vineyard. I share the experiential theology expressed by the composer of hymn 25 in

"Ngoma dze United Methodist Church ye Zimbabwe" Titled: "Ndinoshamiswa kwazvo"

Doh is G

Tune: Synod

{:d.t,ll, :-. r : d . l, ¦ s, :- :- : d . m ¦r :- . f : m. r¦ d:-

1. Ndinoshamiswa Kwazvo
   Namabasa makuru
   Akaitiwa nemi,
   Ose anorumbidza;
   Ukuru hwenyu Mwari
   Hunoshamisa kwazvo.

   I am in awe of
   The great works
   You have done,
   All praise;
   Your greatness, O God
   Is amazing.

2. Kana ndarangira
   Mabasa okudenga
   Kana ndarangarira
   Mabasa apanyika
   Inobuda misodzi
   Kana ndafunga imi

   When I remember your
   Heavenly works
   When I remember your
   Earthly acts
   I weep
   At the thought of you

3. Mwari vatatumumwe,
   Itai timudei;
   Nokuti makatida
   Makazotipa Jesu;
   Matipa Mweya wenyu
   Wokuti simbaradza

   Triune God,
   Three in One;
   Because you loved us
   You gave us Jesus;
   Give us your Spirit
   To strengthen us.

4. Rumbidza iwe denga!   Praise you heaven!
    Rumbidza iwe nyika!   Praise you, O land!
    Rumbidza iwe gungwa!   Praise the sea!
    Nesu ngatirumbidze!   Let us also praise
    Uyu Musiki wedu,   Our Creator,
    Ano rudo rukuru.   And his great love.

Travelling to these different places was according to God's plan for me to gain the experience I needed to serve God Himself and the people. This was the best I could do to please God and fulfil His purpose for my life. Naturally, we all need empowerment – physically, mentally, and spiritually – to function effectively in society for the betterment of people's welfare. Therefore, the church must adopt an ex-fugal (outgoing) approach in its concept of missiology so it may reach out to the church members and the unchurched, for its growth and development.

Church planting and the nurturing of church members requires volunteers who have the passion to do the work faithfully, be they pastors or laity, in obedience to the Lord's Great Commission as stated in Matthew 28:19-20 – *"Therefore go and make disciples of all nations baptising them in the name of the Father and of the Son and of the Holy Spirit, and teach them to obey everything I have commanded you. And surely, I am with you always, to the very end of the age."*

To be effective, one needs spiritual power, given by the Lord, as is clearly stated in John 15:5 – *"I am the vine, and you are the branches. Those who remain in me, and I in them, will bear much fruit, for you can do nothing without me."* Believers in Jesus Christ should endeavour to be disciplined and seek to do the will of God as it is done in heaven. When they miss the target in terms of what they ought to do spiritually and morally, they should return quickly to the Lord and humbly ask for forgiveness to be put right with God the Father, for whom we live.

I am motivated by individuals who have gone before us in faith, who lived sacrificial lives for the sake of the Lord and suffered vicariously for mankind. We must do our best, although our best may not be good in the sight of others. God knows our strengths and weaknesses. All we have to do is to work diligently and faithfully, leaving what we cannot do in the hands of the Lord to accomplish, on our behalf. One of the hymns that has deep spiritual meaning and that uplifts my soul is "I Remember Calvary."

1. Where He may lead me, I will go,
For I have learned to trust Him so,
And I remember 'twas for me,
That He was slain on calvary.

Refrain
Jesus shall lead me night and day,
Jesus shall lead me all the way,
He is the truest friend to me,
For I remember calvary.

2. O I delight in His command,
Love to be led by His dear hand;
His divine will is sweet to me,
Hallowed by blood-stained calvary.

3. Onward I go, nor doubt nor fear,
Happy with Christ my Saviour nearby,
Trusting that I someday shall see,
Jesus my friend of calvary.

The immutability of our God motivates us to do that which is good in His sight and that which helps others, for God is love and fulfils what He promises His people. Hence, God is faithful to Himself. He knows everything, and He is present everywhere. Because God is holy, we should aspire to be holy through faith in Jesus Christ, the perfect One and through whom we can emerge perfect before the throne of God the Father at the end of time.

CHAPTER FOUR

Children's Education

My family educational and motivational acronym is "GEM"

G stands for **God**: Know God as your Lord and worship Him. Seek to do His will.

E stands for **Education**: As much as you can, acquire education to enable you to be an enlightened, productive, and engaged member of society.

M stands for **Money**: Seek money diligently and justly for the proper use, to meet your needs and for the welfare of the people in the society. It is to be spent meaningfully and not to be wasted. Waste not, want not. Learn to save money for future use.

Briefly, this is who I am as an individual, a family member and part of the church, the body of Jesus Christ, and what I believe in. Doing the will of God helps people to co-exist in harmony in the world. The Lord's principle for human existence is LOVE, which can liberate people from all evils. It eliminates vices like hatred, murder, corruption, nepotism, stealing, sexual immorality etc. Let us guard our families jealously against all sorts of evils, and let us all cling to our faith in Jesus for our salvation from sin and eternal death.

Let all believers in God through Jesus keep on remembering the words that were said to those who went before us in faith, "I am the vine; you are the branches, if a man remains in me and I in him, he will bear much fruit; apart from me you can do nothing" (John 15:5). These words should be extended to the unchurched in the world for their good and for the good of others to the glory of God our Maker, in whom we live on Earth. It is God for whom we were created to live, and to whom all people will ultimately go and give their accounts of what they did or did not do, either deliberately or unwittingly. God's judgement will be based on their reports.

Rev. Josephat Chaponda Banda as a Married Man

I am married to Mrs Mavis Banda (nee Nyandowe).

We have nine children together – five sons and four daughters. We have twenty-two grandchildren and two great-grandchildren. We have been married for fifty-four years now.

Mrs M. Banda (Pastors' wives, women's department staff member)

Rev. J. C. Banda and Mrs M. Banda with their nuclear and extended families.

Mrs Mavis Banda's Education and Experience

Mrs Mavis Banda holds a diploma in typing and bookkeeping, a diploma in cutting and advanced designing (Harare Polytechnical College), a diploma in dressmaking (Harare Polytechnical College), and a diploma in education (University of Zimbabwe). She trained at Nyadire Teacher's College, majoring in fashion and fabrics, and later taught student pastors' wives in cutting, designing, and dressmaking. She served as a district women's worker in the Mrewa District of the United Methodist Church in 1989, the Masvingo District of the United Methodist Church from 1997 - 2004, and the Bulawayo Midlands District of the United Methodist Church in 2004. She was an RRW Charge women's worker in the UK North Charge from 2005 - 2009 and the UK Midlands Charge from 2010 - 2020. She was also a Mission Area women's worker for the Missional Area of the UK, Australia, New Zealand, Canada, and the Republic of Ireland from 2015 - 2018. Mrs M. Banda introduced the free conference call prayer-line in the UK in 2014, which is being put into effective use by members of different denominations to this day.

Rev. J. C. Banda and Mrs M. Banda's Children's Education

Mr Mulephere Banda

- B.A. (Hons) History and Religious Studies, University of South Africa
- B.A. (Hons) Development Studies, University of Western Cape
- Diploma in Education

Dr Emmanuel Banda

- B.A. (Hons) and Grad. CE., University of Zimbabwe
- M.S. in College Student Personnel, Miami University (USA)
- PhD. Student Affairs in Higher Education, Miami University (USA)

Mrs Marcia Nkomo

- Diploma in Typing, Harare Polytechnical College

Mr Ransom Banda

- Diploma in Education

Mr Handsome H. Banda

- B.Eng., Aston University (UK)
- M.Sc. in Mechanical Engineering, Aston University (UK)

Mrs D. Banda

- Dressmaking, Cutting and Designing Advanced level, Harare Polytechnical College
- Certificate in Cloth Technology, Masvingo Polytechnical College
- Diploma in Cloth Technology and Pattern making, Mutare Polytech
- Diploma in Education, University of Zimbabwe at Belvedere Teachers' College

Mrs Tisungane Muganiwa

- B.A. Humanities and Social Sciences, Africa University
- Diploma in Human Resources (ZIMPAM)

Mrs Thokozani Chiwara

- B.Sc. Psychology, University of Zimbabwe
- M.Sc. Social Work, University of Wolverhampton (UK)

Mr Shadreck Banda

- B.Sc. Biomedical Sciences, Keele University (UK)
- M.Sc. Biomedical Blood Sciences, Keele University (UK)
- PGDip Physician Associate Studies, University of Wolverhampton (UK)

In conclusion, from my Christian heart, I implore you to be steadfast in your faith and surrender yourselves to the will and service of God. This will allow you to see what I have seen in my life journey, along which I am still travelling to reach my permanent home. You and I are truly images of God (imago Dei), endowed with characteristics and responsibilities of the transcendent God who wants us to be as righteous as He is. He is Immortal, and we are mortal, and yet the Immortal has a plan for the mortal to live forever in the life to come through their faith in Him – the Triune God.

You and I are images that reflect the goodness of the Immortal in thought, word, and deed to please Him. When we sin, we disappoint and anger Him, and when we do good of any kind, we please Him. We are beacons of the invisible reality of the one from whom we came and to whom we are all travelling. Just as Jesus is known as the Alpha and Omega, the First and the Last, the Word that created the universe out of nothing and became flesh for our sake through the Virgin Mary. Confession of our sins in the life journey for the forgiveness of our sins is necessary for our relationship with God to be put right by God Himself when He forgives us. Let's all travel the life journey in faith and with resilience to reach our permanent home safely yonder, beyond the blue sky.

Rev. J.C. Banda and Mrs M. Banda at a wedding of a church member in Bristol, England.

God has plans for us all. Let's cling to our faith in Jesus for a safe end in life.

Experiences During My Retirement So Far

Soon after I retired from active service as an Ordained Minister of the United Methodist Church, the nation experienced a life-threatening and fatal Coronavirus pandemic. We had to take the health-protective measure of lockdown, where people were urged by the government to wear face masks, maintain social distancing and wash and sanitize their hands. In some cases, people were also in self-shielding and self-isolation. History repeats itself but not in the exact manner. Calamities of different kinds happen in life but they are all under the control of our Sovereign God, even if we suffer and lose lives. In the book of Isaiah 26:20, God said, "Go, my people, enter your rooms and shut the door behind you, hide yourselves for a while until His wrath has passed." This is like our lockdown today. God inspires people like scientists, doctors, ministers of religion, nurses, healthcare workers and other frontline workers. They are all under the guidance and protection of God to continue performing their duties even under very difficult conditions. God gives them wisdom, courage, empathy and passion to serve people and the needy as they try hard to save lives through God's help.

God is the Provider of all the things we have. When we find ourselves in hopeless situations, He comes to our aid to show us the way out through the people He sends to curb suffering. He is able to give orders to natural phenomena like the COVID-19 pandemic to stop causing havoc. Remember, God created things out of nothing. He spoke and things came into existence. God wants the people He created in His image to be obedient to Him as He is Holy. Rebellion against God by people kindles His anger, theologically speaking. Let's run away from God's anger and seek to be righteous or to have the right relationship with Him (Genesis 6: 9-19). God does not compromise with sin. When we sin, we should confess our sins to God and ask for forgiveness wholeheartedly and He will forgive us in order to start a new life as forgiven people.

Here are biblical texts of encouragement in times of calamities. Proverbs 3: 25-36; Psalm 91:2, Psalm 46: 1-2; 2 Corinthians 4: 8-9; 2 Corinthians 5:1; Isaiah 43:2, Psalm 27:5; Nahum 1;7; Psalm 93: 4, Matthew 7: 25. Through these texts and others in the Holy Bible, I have been comforted and strengthened to trust in God always. When I live in Jesus, I am a safe living person and if I die believing in Jesus, I am a safe dead person awaiting to be resurrected to live with my Lord eternally.

Praying Ceaselessly – a Christian Helpful Practice

Women, men, boys, girls and people of different denominations have resorted to praying ceaselessly during the COVID-19 pandemic, using the free-conference call prayers early in the morning, 365 days a year. From 05:00hrs to 07:00hrs, they meet in the comfort of their homes reading the Bible, singing hymns, preaching and interceding for people in different difficult situations in the world. When they congregate through telephones, they enjoy their oneness in their worship, even though they are geographically separated and out of sight from one another. They refer to themselves as church members gathering in "the church building without walls wide enough to accommodate many congregants."

These prayer warriors have now extended their times of prayer to cater for those who can meet from 09:00hrs to 10:00hrs, 12:00hrs to 13:00hrs and midnight. Many congregants have testified how their worship has helped them in various aspects of life during these very difficult times as they remain vigilant and prayerful. The worshippers believe strongly that God hears their prayers and answers them at different times. Members of different denominations are free to share the word of God in Shona (Zimbabwean language) and English. They sing their inspiring denominational hymns. Yes, God is at work here. I also attend these prayer meetings.

Mrs Mavis Banda, my wife, initiated this kind of free conference call prayer-line with Mrs Marylyn Maiwasha as an administrator in 2014. It has now spread across England and the Republic of Ireland.

Group members have planned rosters for the preachers and intercessors to pray for different situations in the world, hoping for God to intervene for the welfare of His people. They advocate for love, justice, righteousness and peace in the world through prayers to our omnipresent God who is the God of history. The history we make, we make with Him for if we do good of any kind, He supports us and when we go stray in thought, word and deed, He reminds us and calls us to righteousness. In Matthew 5; 48, we read thus: "Be perfect, therefore, as your heavenly Father is perfect."

Since only God is perfect, believers in Jesus Christ are made perfect through faith in Jesus Christ, the sinless one and the expiation of our sins (Romans 3: 10-26; John 3:16). Prayers comfort those who say them and those for whom they are said. They draw us close to God, the source of all wisdom and our ever-present help in times of trouble on whom we depend for our existence.

In Isaiah 43; 16, we have words of encouragement as believers. *"This is what the Lord says – he who made a way through the sea, a path through the mighty waters."*

Christian Virtues for Morality

It takes faith with the help of the Holy Spirit to acknowledge the existence of our Triune God the Lord of the universe whose grace suffices to all the people in the world (1 Corinthians 12; 3). Some Christian believers fall into apostasy because of troubles of different kinds like ailments, poverty hunger, doubts, joblessness, persecutions, idolatry and immorality.

Blessed are those who try hard to live a clean life and uphold the Christian virtues like love, faith, righteousness, perseverance, hope and courage when confronted by adversity. However, for us Christians, salvation is through faith in Jesus Christ and by God's grace (Ephesians 2: 8-10).

.

CPSIA information can be obtained
at www.ICGtesting.com
Printed in the USA
LVHW070545230222
711710LV00010BA/543

9 781399 911764